W0254390

MOONGARDEN

MOONGARDEN

ANTHONY McCANN

Wave Books
Seattle · New York

Published by Wave Books
www.wavepoetry.com

Wave Books titles are distributed to the trade by
Consortium Book Sales and Distribution
1045 Westgate Drive, St. Paul, Minnesota 55114

Library of Congress Cataloging-in-Publication Data:
McCann, Anthony.
Moongarden / Anthony McCann.-- 1st ed.
p. cm.
ISBN 1-933517-02-6 (pbk. : alk. paper) -- ISBN 1-933517-06-9 (alk. paper)
I. Title.
PS3613.C3453M66 2006
811'.6--dc22
2005023698

Designed and composed by J. Johnson
Printed in the United States of America

9 8 7 6 5 4 3 2 1

First Edition

Wave Books 003

for Ellen

Contents

Moongarden (November)

On the eve of the wedding
        the witch arrived in the city

      the great lawn

plunged
          into dark
and silent pleasure

In the public forest

a man
entered the body

of a stranger

When it happened
           his eyes were closed

his right hand blooms

in cold November

           night cars

are converted
into light

In the distance:

recorded sounds
of ventilation

and the sea

There is no damage
to the liquid

while you sleep

the earth leaks
cold traffic

onto the street

And the city?

What did the city do?

It made happiness
and codes

in the windows underground

I left my voice
inside your body

when I drowned

Ode to the Lake

I, myself, should have been a thing.

But then the things themselves appeared.

Some were called the squibs.

Others, vague and old,
became the higher animals.

They were like

words painted in the lake
or like

clouds riddled through with sun.

And also they were like
some more directions to the builders.

It's true—I should have grown protective gear.

But whether I woke up in the park
smeared in pink and yellow thread

or when I walked around the lake
damaging the geese

I stayed exactly how I am.

So when I rush along the world
it leaves a rushing in my ears

and I am placed along the water
as the lake becomes a thing.

Holy Week

Once I woke up with three of them on me
two holding my arms
the third, their captain, had its snout in my face.
I can still hear its breathing.
Which is when loneliness entered my body.
When I woke again they were gone.
The mountains were deeply mislabeled in sun.
A human child stood over me
holding a small, blood-flecked stone.
I returned to the cantina which was not a cantina
but merely a window
onto the street where I stood.
Or where I had stood.
"O, darkness mine, etc.," I prayed.
And then darkness fell directly from the air.
Next morning the town was in plain fiesta.
A man—one human man—
made a symbol with his rubber hands.
He was symbolizing me.
Together we stood in the plaza
over the ashes
where Judas Iscariot
had been exploded in the plaza.
All that was left was his head.
Instead of a head he had a striped plastic ball
and instead of a face he had two dots and a mouth.
The next day was Sunday.
When I woke the Lord was already risen.

The pigs next door were eating a shoe
or some other kind of human face.
Who will there be to forgive them when I die?
Monday I left town on the back of a truck
blowing bloody snot into the back of my hat—
dawn blasting the high plains
with the cold damage of light forever.

Moongarden

Because the moon is his most important organ
Max is obliged to conceal it in his body.
It is the source of his eternal youth.
According to Max the moon is falling
All the way through our bodies
To the bottoms of our soles. When it gets there
We are history. Meanwhile
Max is tortured by women—
By some sad and beautiful women.
Because Max is not his name.
In the Moongarden they proffer their cheeks
For the final kiss, the kiss goodbye.
In his first photos of the coffin academy
Young Max exhibits a flair for light.
Light and potable, the portable moon
Feeds itself on Max.
Though she be round of face
And worshipped by Max
She will not return.
Enter Max on a bright disc of snow
Which the moon is obliged to reflect.
O Milky Moon, Mammalian Moon,
The Moon of Failure, the Human Moon.
According to The Poet—{*Enter The Poet*}—
The moon is not like anything—
The moon is just the moon.
According to Max the moon is a map:
A lifesize map of the moon.

Woe to the Wildebeest, Whose Flesh is to be Torn

They are not horses, they are large
and shaggy scholars. Sometimes
they look dignified and great.
Their voice is the voice of
certain frogs, a species
of enormous croaking.
Wildebeest, exact and sober Wildebeest!
Defrocked Franciscans, they roam the plains
teaching the grasses to sing and
to ejaculate. They are not hyenas, they
are Wild Dogs. Beneath the surface of the plains
they hunt cocaine
and the elusive Wildebeest.
In their features we see the features of
other creatures:
The Downy Woodpecker,
The Humpbacked Whale.
The Wildebeest ejaculate.
They are heavy-headed mammals and
it makes them sad,
it makes them hang their heads
which gives them a formal air
during lectures and group discussions.
Their stamping and their waste
discipline and rejuvenate the grass.
It's been years since the Gods
took away their pants.

They are not badgers—
they are Wild Dogs. They are
great kissers and experts.
They are specialists
in refrigeration. At night
they burrow
beneath the plains
in the fevered hunt
of fresh cocaine. At dawn
they seek the Wildebeest.

Los Lectores Pueden Poner El Título Que Quieran a Este Poema

And here I am Mother, slick haired and heaving
A kind of elk, something, a sort of human elk
Digitally inserted into the prehistory of his nation
Twenty feet tall and roaring and extinct

Mother, I'm a mammal, when I'm sleeping I'm exuding
As the little pony reaches the shimmering pines
Here I am Mother, struggling to hear
Here's my new body, made wholly of hair

Mother, here I am, a grown man in the snow
Mother, the dark here is sort of enormous
As the little pony passes through the sacred meadows
Here I am holding the breasts of my wife

Twenty feet tall and roaring and extinct
The dark here, Mother, is truly enormous
As the little pony enters the shimmering pines
Dear Mother, I'm a mammal, in love with the pines

Arthur Rimbaud

Last night I dreamt of the parkway again
The Senators: silent, dignified, sad
The Sky: blue as the eyes of the beast
I ripped off his ear and part of his face

After the accident he began to smell different
Not badly exactly, he began to smell sweet
I wrote a letter explaining my motives
I lined up each pill on the mantel by color

The lines are cut, the shades are drawn
Our bodies are factories factoring light
Our bodies were factories delivering light
I was wearing a raincoat and red leather pants

In the sky the city had been detained
I was locked in the bathroom spitting up foam
Later I helped him search the lawn for his teeth
The Whole Sky was a flag: blue and horribly still

Ode to the Sky

It was the color that lived in a horse—
An epidemic of lost rocks.

Then the sun came and struck the rocks
And I stood with the others and I looked at the sky

To which one cloud was pinned
Because the sky and its color are things.

This is the history of that weather.
It's an ode to schizophrenia.

O Schizophrenia, it says,
You are like the weather—

A coincidence of symptoms
And the name of The Disease.

In the shade of that obscenity
I pretend to be a tree,

A practitioner of Human Studies
And all the other science, because

This is what my limbs are for:
To make these circles in the grass.

This is what my lips are for:
Replacing all the words.

To the American Poets

Colonel, while a captain, you became my father, in a radiant field
Gentle evening, biblical, and imported from Peru
You touched my father's dappled edge, you made my father dappled
And the deer at the edge of evening, these are French, translucent deer

Dear evening, you make me think of them, these deer, and science
And those dogs, dead dogs, murdered dogs, in plastic bags
I'm talking about torture in the Republic of Vermont
(Dear evening: gentle torture, I'm talking about youth)

MY YOUTH, My youth in radiance, near the academy of torture
A field of cheese, Dear evening: you are a field of cheese
I have seen your heart, your heart beating, your heart is dark and beating
And at the center of each torture, the forest stays cool and wet

O Colonels of the forest of the American School of Torture!
(I have seen these colonels, people, I have seen these people sleep)
And the frothing fronds of an uncountable fern
"Everything has been seen, lords / through the eyes of my horse"

Radiance Through Fascism

I want to write a poem for the land
To make people weep and fall in love with the land

With the edge of the forest, exact and alone
With the light on the ice, soft and exact

And I want to learn how to die in this light
In this deliberate air, in this deliberate light

And I don't want to write any beautiful poems
That are the sweet resurrection of lyrical pictures

And I want to kiss you all on your fingers
(Your fingers are real from holding the snow!)

And I want to go back to the North,
And I want to restore the North to the North
And make people weep and fall in love with the North

(And, discretely, I want to redeem the land)

Irish Rep

We'd harnessed seal force in this
piece about the sea.

It's about
Moving in the sea. It's a video

About the animals that live here.

And blowing air
Out through our holes. It's

An award-winning film
About your body. It all

Takes place in that
Secret land

Whose splendors
Have now

Been lost. Where men
Burn the blessèd earth and

Drink to blind delight
In the

Always present cloud

That hangs at
Just about their knees. It is

A refrigerated cloud.
Which is how the future comes

To the Green Island
Bar and Grill: When Someone

Sleeping on the floor
Wakes up! It's all a dream

About this house.
I don't know where

To put
50 Bright White Envelopes

On the table
Dressed in lace. As I said,

It's not my house.

3/17/03

I wonder if my corpse turns orange.
Is this tea made of tea? Do ankles rot?
O. I'm just another kid
In the drunken crowd.
But if there's one thing more
I want to do in this lifetime it's
Barefoot Pilgrimage. Imagine it:
One bright drop of
Green beer
On the forehead
Of the penitentiary. O. Shame: it's
Syncretic, people. People, it's
Lymphatic. It scalds
The insides of the skin.
And, people, I swear to you
It makes me useful.

The Temptations

Now you will feel absolutely terrified
And you are burning
And you will want to drink a beer
A gallon of beer immediately
And some water
Then you will want water
You are under the command of water completely
And you are absolutely terrified
This has been your experience
You put your face between your knees
You put your hands behind your head
You are under arrest
Under the command of science
You will be sentenced to the stars
To hard labor on the stars
On the surface of the stars
In a scientific suit
Of unmeltable plastics
Chilled with dry ice
And with some other kind of ice

(Rats will watch you from the moon
And you will want to drink a beer)

*

And you will want to speak
But under the command of water
All the verbs are swimming
And you are kneeling in the water
And you are receiving your commands
That are the commands of science
To free the gases of the stars
And you are absolutely terrified
And you will want to speak

*

Now a horse appears
Under the command of science
It is Horses on the Stars
It has come to cut your name

*

With a vision should come pain

A horse represents the pain
You may not give it as a gift
And you may not accept it
And you will have to buy it

*

This has been your experience
Under the command of water
The desert will suddenly bloom
The surface of the stars will bloom
And all the stars will drown
And you will have drowned the stars
And you will be absolutely terrified
That maybe really you are burning

Querida Managua,

1.

Dear Managua, What are horses?
Are they ponies? Fathers?
Ponyfathers?
Are they penises?
Or are they simply cars?
Do they represent the sky?
Or the opposite of sky?
Do they breathe?
What happens to their bodies
when the rain covers up their legs?
Do they exist, Managua?
Managua, are they burning?

2.

Managua, the helicopters are burning
                    The private   helicopters are burning

          Little birds are falling, baby birds are crashing

   Falling in my inner patio

   It's the high season of the air, the main epoch of the wind

And, Managua, everything is burning

Because everything can burn

The animals are falling

Since anything can fall

3.

Would you rather be a pony or a ghost, Managua?
Am I on my knees? Are these my knees?
Is this a raindrop
Or a leaf ? Who cut down the trees?
Who took my dirt?
What was the value of the dirt?
The taken dirt?
And the Milk
the color of dirt
that all our drinking was about?
Will I be reimbursed?
Who took the milk, Managua?
What happened to the moon?

4.

Estimada Managua,

this morning there were some explosions in the clouds
against all regulations of the clouds
governing explosions in the clouds
In the subsequent scandal dawn was exposed

and is now being represented
by the surface of the clouds
as a series of small diaphanous dents

5.

And they are fucking us, Managua

This very night
That is not the night
That is the body
That is not your body
That is the night
Inside your body
This very night

They are fucking our mothers

6.

Attn: Managua
This has been my impact report
On how I have impacted you
I sent it to my self
Dear Gov't, it said,
Managua does not exist
O, Managua
The arrival of the rains has been a grand consolation
Today I found a lizard in my bath

Why does he tremble so?
Is he afraid of me Managua?
Or is he scared of you?

7.

And if all the horses stay like this?
tied as they are to the speed of traffic
And if all the ponies fall?
Drink from this cup Managua
Listen to the engine in the floor

Miami International Airport Hotel

1.

The alarm goes off—I'm still in the airport. Is it impossible to imagine my physical shape? I was dreaming of jobs again and of t-shirts that scream "Chicago!" And then I am absent, suddenly, accepting the fact: it remains impossible to imagine this hotel.

Are we inside the airport or are we clinging to its ribs?

At the elevator bank the walls are locked. The air piped in on rods of dust.

The doors open onto a square of grass.

To my right and to my left: two bright and empty hours.

2.

The alarm goes off. I'm still here. I awake feeling a pang of support for the locally grown organic foods movement. After so long of being unable to move. The walls here fit together perfectly and are slathered with mirrors. But when I go to the window it's the same view of a vague and depthless dark. Is the hotel inside the window or is it grafted to its face? I fall asleep. The alarm goes off.

*

The hotel is drawn to exigent specifications that required the installation of these massive mirrors. The mirrors are where the walls get locked. (The dark behind the mirrors is where they brew the air.)

*

The restaurant is seamlessly integrated into the hotel system of the airport and is called simply "The Port" or, alternately, "The Port View Restaurant." On the roof there is a finely trimmed lawn, the grass slick with halogen light. From here I see a blue disc moving in the dark. This is a New World Presentation.

3.

I should have been a blue disc.
In my dream I was sleeping.
Retaining some sort of physical shape.
A hollow hot place in the middle of the deep.
I was in this hotel but this hotel in Chicago
as the doors opened in a perfect yawn.
But out there in the dark, man,
they grow things you never seen—plastic
wrists, witches made of glass.
Meanwhile I wake panting, sleeping on my waist.
The hotel has no shape and is never dark inside—
the dark is outside between the mirrors and my skin
while the hotel is drawn to demanding exceptions.

At this point a new motif is introduced:
fossils encrusted in the airport linoleum.
I am drawn to re-imbedding in the surface of the place.
Where for this air, these robot tunes?
This has been a New World Presentation.

Robert Stone

The pure products
Of America
Love Math
And Radiance
Want

A Real Relationship
With Divine

Substance
And are all

Criminals.
The head

Of Rubén Darío
Is not
Their toy.
It is only

Half boiled.
Fever

Plus Gin
Equals Fever.

Translucent
North American

Lawn Networks

Vanish
At the edge
Of your fever.

You

Are an agent.
In your photo

The edges
Of your photo
Are burning.

These
Are your objectives:

1. Expansion
2. Reduction and

3. More Fever. Put your hand
On the glowing salt
On the surface
Of the desert. Put your face
On the glowing
Desert of Salt. Here
Where a waste
Of cinders

Slopes down

The absence
Of mercy
Is terrific.

Incidents of Travel

Dawn: a body   stuffed with guests

bald high plains and
Suddenly!

Flamingoes taking flight
        across the frozen salt

Guardrail by guardrail
the army is stealing this country

      In the ruddy light   stained with cold
  a magnet broods

 in the unfrozen guts

      The earth leaks ink
on the horse path and shoes

   Are you human   or a ghost?
someone asks

but he is only speaking

casting glamour
                    down the cracks

One light on: a man selling hearts on skewers

                                                Somehow
we arrived at a cave

"The river"
                                "seems stiller "

"at night "

     "with the torches"

was the only thing
    I ever said to our leader

There was really nothing else to believe in

        My racist thoughts raced over the plains
over the feed lots and the legions of sod

                On the floor

the city
was glowing like creation

        and the sidewalks
were covered with bluish bird pulp
                                        When I entered the lobby

my legs were still trembling

Some animals
were sneaking

down
into the rust

It was danger
gave them life
but damage
makes us shine

Sonnet

February 25th   1643
I'm alone in the McDonalds, you don't love me
Begins the Ballad of Johnny Coyne
"I was a vivid burgher/No Europe could restrain"
Guardians of the eastern doorway, people of the stone
Must be born and reborn to belong
(Ellen knocks and reenters the poem   Hello Ellen)
I step in the stream, but the water has moved on
At 18th Avenue and again, here, at Avenue P
I am the rare and livid Willem Kieft!
Returning as Romans victorious from Gaul
The CIA gave me acid   Now I can't die
O Guardians of the eastern door
There is no way back to the sky

F Train to Avenue X

From Fort Hamilton Parkway
All the way to Avenue X
Fatherhood reduces Brooklyn to pure geometry
At 18th Avenue and again, here, at Avenue P
Only the dead know Fatherhood
Gathered at the window, counting beads of light
Fatherhood is the last warm thing in your hands
I have to say something about Fatherhood:
Fatherhood replaces England
So that no one may look into it
So that no one may hold it up to the sky
All the way to Gravesend, last night I rode the F
Fatherhood rode by the window
I took the F train back to jail

Ode to the Sky (Seattle)

Science fills the sky
with radiant description.

Splendid weather:
thin clouds running toward the west.
          Bright rivers
drain the silver land.

     But I will keep talking
until your breasts appear
again, inside this chamber,
and to me alone.

I remember:

we were sitting on this iron bench
above the north south interstate.

All my nerves
were stuffed
deep into your pants.

Behind us
the sky turns green, then gray
and pink and black.

This memory, recovered
by myself

working alone
without the guidance
of licensed professionals
just this very afternoon,

may not bear up under
cross-examination.

But I know the sky was blind

and my extremities were trembling.

Some nights
I stayed up all night
eating little clouds.

Later, you woke up
and started fucking me again.

And still later,
you came back to me.

December

The devil poured
    the light

                                        of all his body
 into a single

silver coin

    I feel the light
of whisky
                            pouring

 through my feet

On a road from childhood:

                            the rich
and frozen dirt

and the sound
   of a row

of birches
in the snow

Holding you
I see our bones

            and blood

replaced with stars

                        or blue
thinly
            star like things

The purple trees

are thinly drawn
against

the witchy
space

The window

fingerlicks
the frost
            Indoors
I am a blur

You are a blur

            I'd like to be a shape

I take your body
in my mouth

The ridge
is plump

with the wrinkly shapes
of froze-up roots
            and things:

            the lost bodies
of the higher gnomes

The deer
have burrowed on

into the center
of the world

In December

the blue blue
billy goat

fell
            deep

into the treasure

Hope and Damage
            rode my heart

into the gentle waste

Moongarden (The Enchanted Prince)

Since I have been a child again
I have imagined the president sleeping
I have imagined the president is lost
having walked out alone from his cabin in the mountains
early early before anyone woke
and now suddenly the light is fading
and he's been walking in circles for hours
earlier, toward noon, he saw several rabbits
and later, around 3 maybe, he saw a fox
but now there are only crowds
the president has forgotten everything about people
or the secret motives of other people
or this is how he imagines himself
it is the president's best idea to panic
panic in his body is a small blue fluid
but when the president seeks the Useful Life
through the Powers of Concentration and Positive Thought
Logos touches the president's hair
and his hair turns to crumpled up paper
this happens only at night
when the central city has been abandoned
and the traffic lights click and grind
and the president is dreaming of the parkway again
in his dream he cannot iron his clothes
in truth the president is not authorized to learn
sometimes I think it might only hurt him
when Brilliant Logos touches his hair
meanwhile in the forest the lights have gone out

the fox studies science in his luminous lair
and panic sleeps in the eyes of a mouse
in the president's palace the dark carpets brood
and the floors seemed greased with oily light
I draw circles around his body thrice
and hope to forgive my dreadful thoughts
my thoughts about you dear reader
you alone with your dreadful thoughts
as the moon rises gently over the antique park
and the earth smells sweet and artificial

November

Sudden woodlands demand our attention.
Pain arrives next in a red handled thing.

And from over the hill the liquid running of drums!
As a swan parts the water and buries its fist!

This is some kind of serious facility.
The air: a bad ship: bottling gusts.

No one will call it a miracle.
No one will ever eat me again.

Percoset

I.

In the last moment

Of the Bill of Rights

For two hours
I was made of cream

In the distance: a shimmering sweat

Now more than ever
I'm aware of living here

2.

I love when the suckerfish sucks on the astronaut
I love when the suckerfish sucks on the moon

When my Phantom Jet is sleeping
My Phantom Jet is fighting

A bright and dreamless sleep
In a high gravity place

In Favor of One's Time

my clear
plastic cup
was creased
with milky veins

wet lights
hung loose
along the grammar
of the hills

each day
the death count
was revised

alone sometimes
in pairs
we canvassed
the terrain

near me always
was a highway
and the silent power
of the birds

the cry the song
finds limits

but my body
is a vessel
of their joy

Greatest Snow Emergency Ever

Coming in, coming out,
of distant music

I make a point of
not speaking
because

right now

I am typing (I have no
body people,

                              people, here I am)

*

And when we wake up
with 2 feet of snow

on my breasts

I say (to myself since I
am always speaking)

I say

This is a nice little shrine

*

I say

Distant music
isn't always

sacred. People

when you wake up (and I'm gone)

it's the Greatest

Snow Emergency Ever

Oda a la Vanguardia

12 minutes later
the clouds

shifted west

shot out
over the harbor

and drowned

joy

in the city
is caused

on the roof

most moods
(made with eyes)
are away

in the distance

the harbor

tosses
black hats

they say
in their bodies
is love

on my body

life glitters

like dots

through the silver
most beautiful

sheets

square buildings
bark
like a face

at night
with square lights
after rain

the city's
a heavy

blue druid

o infinite friends!
at high speeds!

the great streets
were all empty
                    of flags

ice
                                                  on the wings

made me plunge

on our faces
light trembles

like plates

The New Romantics

The Crimes of Science are inexact.

Butterflies suffer in crystalline
Syntax. Nightbirds don't whistle

They crack. Unbreakable

As the sea. O. You.
Unsoilable,

Unsayable,

X!

And what was I waiting to reach you for?
A stranger slept in my ear.

These unpaintable trains—
They have this failure to glisten.

So again I missed the clouding up
Of the cloudless air again.

Forgive me, Doctor, I am spiteful, unclean
And I fear that I might be in rebellion.

When I struggle to be a hero to my people
And near me nothing is burning

Suddenly little circles are burning
And then everyone ignores my radiance.

Rains come to unbutton the air.
The hillsides come unstitched.

Nightbirds creep
            The eaves of this
Ceremonial stone.

As all around us
A void thickens.

Breaking Away

The Lake quakes under the heavy visage
of some really bright red toast.

When you drive into its mouth
it's like driving into handlessness.

This image is unreceivable.

The weather here is just changeable regret.

But I have unmasked the trainer.
And now I wear the trainer's mask.

The Consolation of Literature

Afterwards, when they went out,
There was not a soul on the esplanade.
The sky was thick with birds
And this thickness was called night.
Across the glazed surface of an emerald pool
The sun of the landlord poled his canoe.
We were cold under it, despite my hands—
Their enormity and weather.
"They went out and left us here
with the abstracted air of a disavowed lump.
They will hang their eyes on the moon!"
And so, drowned the moment we are born
That very evening at the class party
The rendered sky, flat and ripped,
Was the color in the ides of science.
O Sky, how can you be so ingenuous?
A vessel in the form of a cup, of great
Diameter and little depth.
How will I ever reconcile
My randy heart
To your ten million blips?
Thus our radiance is reviled.
But as dawn approached with its artful leaks
The vast, likeable air grew thin.
Its glittering is The Miracle of Grammar.

October

It becomes
a stranger's hand

this green and yellow light

when
with sudden tenderness
it touches

the unrecorded edge

of an even
stranger ear

At dusk

beneath the park
a globe of ice is growing
          shot through

with milky flaws
and riddled

with recorded sounds

The trees

raise their squirrely fists

to the plump

and ashy
space

and the harbor
writes itself

in slate

between the fishes
and the sky

In October
baseball
grows dense and solemn

beneath the sea

we watch ourselves

behind the glass

more tiny
on the floor

than we had known

Leaves, leaves   night
shadows of the leaves

these shapes and others
move across your face

in a room lit by
                                        the underwater noise

of corrected

                    sound recordings

But unlike you
I love happiness

and I know you'll make me happy

Tonight
while you were out

I watched a true event
on national TV

Shadows crossed the stadium

The listing crowd
in shining coats

awoke

and began to groan

               as October

pierced their bodies

As it gets colder
every night

the windows of the planets

get curtly
individual

along the park
the buildings
               like pale
sententious apes

watch our bodies

on the frosted grass

Sometime

all this beauty
will have to end

            but not before

the drugs have entered us
and stopped

with sudden tenderness
just above my knees

On the roof
we watched a sermon
            in the sky

the night

drew a cloud
of ashy fluff

across the body
of the moon

and the moon

returned
            relieved

of all its thoughts

This strangeness
to be me alive
is it different
than the one you have?

The cops
filed out
            onto the field
and the stadium

grew loud

            and blue
and empty

But when I woke

it was snowing

and I had no memories

Notes

"Holy Week" samples James Tate's poem "I am Still a Finn."

"The Temptations" includes a line in which rats watch a "you" from the moon. This image comes from the Bolivian poet Jaime Saenz's poem "Homenaje a La Epilepsia."

"Querida Managua," and its author owe a debt to the work of César Vallejo in general, and in particular to one poem, "España, Aparta De Mi Este Cáliz." "Querida Managua," is also indebted to Jaime Saenz and his book-length poem "La Noche." There are echoes and twists of translation from both Vallejo and Saenz in different sections of the poem. There is also a twisted translation of one line of Roque Dalton's poem "Los Extranjeros" in the sixth section.

The poem "Robert Stone" owes much to Robert Stone and, clearly, to William Carlos Williams as well.

Two lines in "Oda a La Vanguardia" are altered translations of a poem by the somewhat mysterious Chilean "vanguardist" poet Omar Caceres.

Acknowledgments

Some of these poems have appeared or will appear in the following journals/magazines: *Forklift, Ohio; Fence; Crowd; jubilat; Incliner* and *H_NGM_N.* The author would like to express his gratitude to all the editors. Thanks also to any publications and their corresponding editors who published or agreed to publish any of these poems after the author had his last chance to thank them here.

The author wishes to acknowledge the thoughtful readings, enthusiasm and advice of the following people during the writing and organization of this book: Ellen Sharp, Matt Rohrer, Sam Witt, Joshua Beckman, Kevin McCann, Mark Allen, and Matthew Zapruder. Thanks to Charlie Wright, the publisher of Wave, and the whole staff of Wave: Lori Shine, Monica Fambrough, Mr. Beckman and Mr. Zapruder. Thanks also to all the other friends who read and gave advice on individual poems now in the book. Thanks to all the organizers who have invited me to read or arranged readings for me. Special thanks to Sherrie Flick, Matt Hart, and Joel Craig. The author also must single out Machine Project of Los Angeles and Mark Allen for endless thanks for all the events and the home away from home.